U.S. SEISMIC ZONES

THE PUERTO RICO TRENCH

DANIELLE HAYNES

PowerKiDS press

Published in 2026 by The Rosen Publishing Group, Inc.
2544 Clinton Street, Buffalo, NY 14224

First Edition

Editor: Danielle Haynes
Book Design: Michael Flynn

Photo Credits: Cover VicPhotoria/Shutterstock.com; (series background) Picksell/Shutterstock.com; pp. 5, 6 zelvan/Shutterstock.com; p. 7 zombiu26/Shutterstock.com; p. 9 Javier Cruz Acosta/Shutterstock.comn; p. 11 DestinaDesign/Shutterstock.com; p. 12 FOTOKITA/Shutterstock.com; p. 13 Designua/Shutterstock.com; p. 15 https://commons.wikimedia.org/wiki/File:Correo_y_Casino_de_Mayag%C3%BCez_luego_del_terremoto_de_1918.jpg; p. 16 https://commons.wikimedia.org/wiki/File:EV_Nautilus.jpg; p. 17 https://commons.wikimedia.org/wiki/File:Expl1196_-_Flickr_-_NOAA_Photo_Library.jpg; p. 19 Alberto Loyo/Shutterstock.com; p. 21 Jason Busa/Shutterstock.com; p. 22 https://commons.wikimedia.org/wiki/File:USS_Milwaukee_(CL-5)_off_New_York_City,_circa_in_August_1943_(19-N-51513).jpg; p. 23 https://commons.wikimedia.org/wiki/File:Atlantic-trench.JPG; p. 25 https://commons.wikimedia.org/wiki/File:Limiting_Factor_at_the_Cumberland_East_Bay_(South_Georgia_Island).jpg; p. 27 NASA's Goddard Space Flight Center; p. 29 Jacob Boomsma/Shutterstock.com.

Cataloging-in-Publication Data

Names: Haynes, Danielle.
Title: The Puerto Rico Trench / Danielle Haynes.
Description: Buffalo, New York : PowerKids Press, 2026. | Series: U.S. seismic zones | Includes glossary and index.
Identifiers: ISBN 9781499453386 (pbk.) | ISBN 9781499453393 (library bound) | ISBN 9781499453409 (ebook)
Subjects: LCSH: Submarine trenches--Juvenile literature. | Plate tectonics--Juvenile literature. | Puerto Rico--Juvenile literature. | Seismology--Juvenile literature.
Classification: LCC GC87.6 H38 2026 | DDC 577.7'9--dc23

Manufactured in the United States of America

CPSIA Compliance Information: Batch #CSPK26. For further information contact Rosen Publishing at 1-800-237-9932.

CONTENTS

WELCOME TO PUERTO RICO

Sitting right in the middle of the clear-blue Caribbean Sea is the U.S. territory of Puerto Rico. This self-governing island is actually an archipelago, a chain of 142 islands of various sizes. Looking at a map, they're located right below a **geological** feature important to the archipelago's formation—the Puerto Rico Trench.

An ocean trench is a long, narrow depression, or sunken area, on the seafloor. They occur near where tectonic plates meet. The Puerto Rico Trench is 1,090 miles (1,750 km) long and 60 miles (100 km) wide. It runs along the northern coast of the main island of Puerto Rico. It also marks the boundary between the North American plate to the north and the Caribbean plate to the south.

The Puerto Rico Trench began forming during the Cenozoic Era, about 66 million years ago.

SUBDUCTION ZONE

There are multiple ways tectonic plates come together. The Puerto Rico Trench was formed by what is called a subduction zone. That means one plate is slipping under another plate as they move. In this case, the Caribbean plate and the North American plate mostly slide past each other. But in this area, the North American plate is subducting underneath the Caribbean plate.

EARTH-SHAKING FACT!

This type of subduction zone, where the two tectonic plates slide past each other instead of crashing directly into one another, is called an **oblique** subduction zone.

The point where one plate subducts under another creates a trench.

When one plate subducts under another, pressure builds up between the two plates, which are locked together. When enough pressure builds up, the top plate will slide against the other suddenly, causing an earthquake. Subduction can also cause a volcanic eruption. When sediment and water from the subducting plate push down into the Earth's hot mantle, it melts the rocks, creating **magma**. The magma gathers and rises to the surface, causing an eruption.

VOLCANOES

The islands of Puerto Rico began to form about 190 million years ago as volcanoes. Today, these volcanoes are extinct, or dead, and are covered by younger, sedimentary rocks. The volcanoes that make up Puerto Rico were last active about 30 million years ago.

As underwater volcanoes erupt, the **lava** they release cools and hardens, creating new landmass. Over time, this landmass will sometimes grow big enough to break the surface of the ocean and create a new island.

When it first formed, the Puerto Rican archipelago was much farther south than it is today. Over millions of years, the island arc was slowly pushed northward and eastward. This happened because the newly forming Caribbean plate moved the North American and South American plates.

El Yunque, one of the tallest mountains in Puerto Rico, is what's left of an extinct supervolcano called Hato Puerco.

JANE K. WILLENBRING AND EL YUNQUE

The work of geologist and Stanford University professor Jane K. Willenbring has given scientists a greater understanding of El Yunque. One of the tallest mountains in Puerto Rico, it's the centerpiece of El Yunque National Forest.

Scientists have wondered why this mountain doesn't **erode** as much as they expect. Willenbring and a team of scientists used technology to study the chemical makeup of El Yunque. They found that the mountain is the remains of a supervolcano that "cooked" the rocks longer than the surrounding landscape, making it stronger.

EARTHQUAKES

Even though Puerto Rico no longer has active volcanoes, it still experiences many earthquakes thanks to the subduction zone. The territory records thousands of earthquakes each year, though most are so small you can't feel them.

Some earthquakes are stronger than others. Scientists measure them using the moment magnitude scale. The higher the number of magnitude, the stronger an earthquake is. Each point on the magnitude scale represents a 10-time increase in strength. So, a 6.5-magnitude earthquake is 10 times more powerful than a 5.5-magnitude earthquake. On average, earthquakes with a magnitude of 6 or greater happen once every 38 years in Puerto Rico. One of the island's most destructive earthquakes on record—with a magnitude of 7.1—happened in 1918.

MOMENT MAGNITUDE SCALE

CATEGORY	MAGNITUDE	DESCRIPTION	HOW COMMON WORLDWIDE?
micro	less than 2.0	Not felt, but recorded by scientific tools	1.4 million a year
minor	2.0 to 2.9	Sometimes felt, rarely cause damage	1.3 million a year
light	3.0 to 3.9	Often felt, rarely causes **significant** damage	130,000 a year
moderate	4.0 to 4.9	Noticeable shaking, significant damage unlikely	13,000 a year
strong	5.0 to 5.9	Can cause significant damage to buildings	1,300 a year
major	6.0 to 6.9	Significant damage in populated areas	100 a year
great	7.0 and higher	Serious damage	10 to 20 times a year

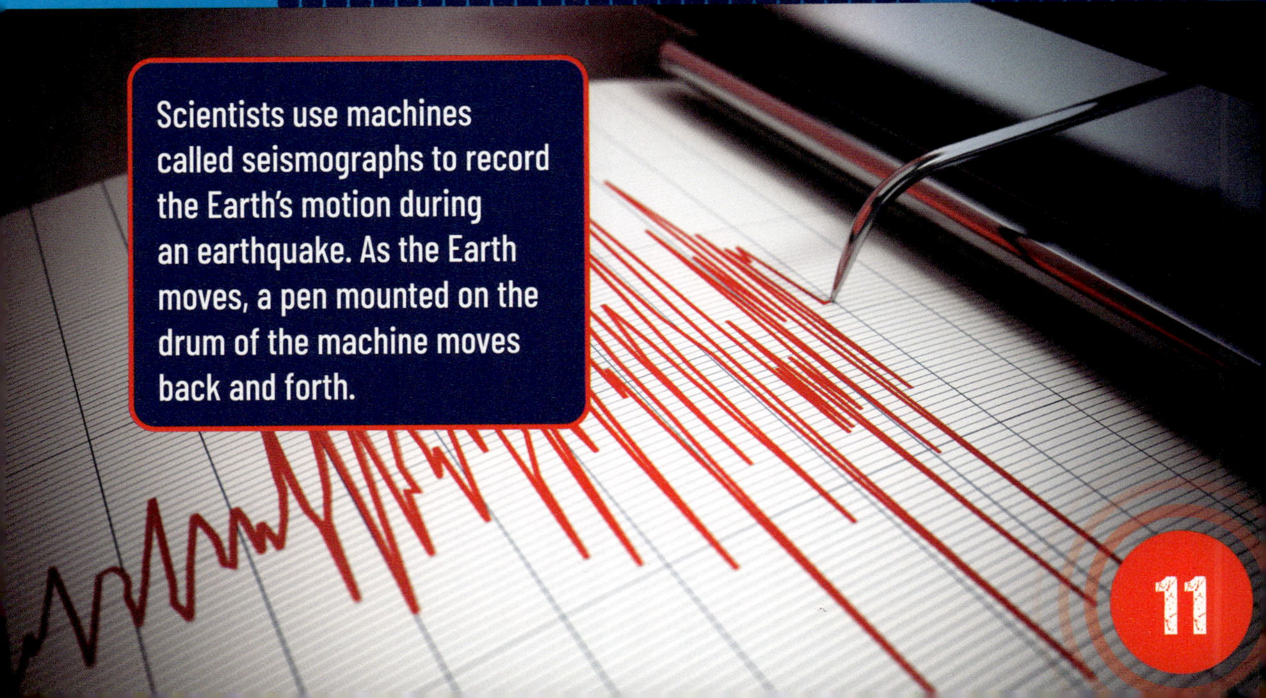

Scientists use machines called seismographs to record the Earth's motion during an earthquake. As the Earth moves, a pen mounted on the drum of the machine moves back and forth.

TSUNAMIS

Sometimes the most dangerous part of an earthquake is what comes after. Seismic activity can trigger a tsunami. This is a large wave that comes from the sea onto land. Most tsunamis are only about 10 feet (3 m), but some can be monstrous.

EARTH-SHAKING FACT!

The largest recorded tsunami happened in Lituya Bay, Alaska, in 1958. It was more than 1,700 feet (518 m) in height!

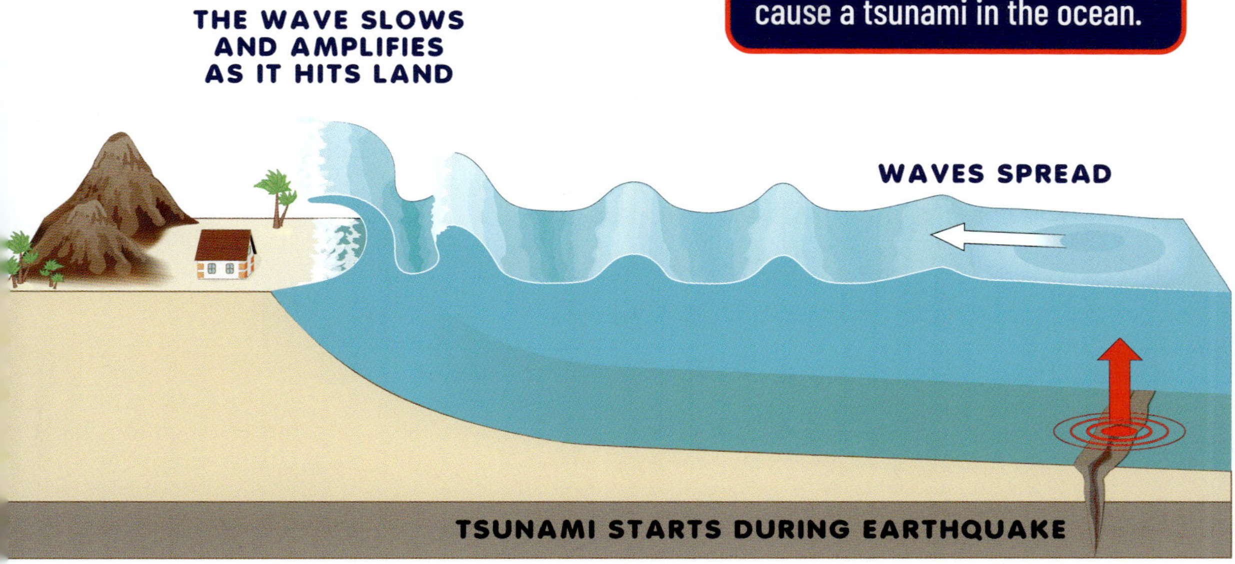

This illustration shows how an underwater earthquake can cause a tsunami in the ocean.

Tsunamis happen when the ocean floor moves vertically. During an earthquake, the top **tectonic** plate breaks free and lifts up. This sudden vertical motion creates a wave in the water. Any kind of earthquake can cause a tsunami, but subduction zone earthquakes create the largest.

Volcanoes can also cause tsunamis, though they're not very common. If a volcano erupts near land or close to the surface of the ocean, it can displace the water enough to create a tsunami. These tsunamis tend to be relatively weak.

1918 SAN FERMÍN EARTHQUAKE

The 7.1-magnitude San Fermín earthquake struck Puerto Rico around 10:14 a.m. on October 11, 1918. The **epicenter** of the quake was located off the northwest coast of the main island in the Mona Canyon, which connects to the Puerto Rico Trench. It was one of the most destructive quakes in the island's history, killing 116 people and causing millions of dollars in damage.

The earthquake also triggered a tsunami with waves up to 20 feet (6 m) high. This, alone, was responsible for 40 of the deaths that day. Witnesses said they first saw the seawater retreat, exposing parts of the seafloor they'd never seen. The water then returned with large, damaging waves.

Most large earthquakes are followed by **aftershocks**. Puerto Rico had aftershocks from the 1918 quake for nine months.

EARTH-SHAKING FACT!

Aftershocks are usually weaker than the main event, but one on October 24, 1918, was strong enough to knock down more buildings.

The earthquake destroyed the post office in Mayagüez.

In 2008, scientists **theorized** that an underwater landslide caused the 1918 earthquake and following tsunami. They came to this conclusion because cables lying under the ocean were broken near the site of where a large landslide had taken place.

However, new research in 2023 found that the landslide in question was too old to be related to the 1918 event. A scientific team led by U.S. Geological Survey (USGS) scientist Uri ten Brink used a remotely operated vehicle to map the landslide and take samples of sediment for **radiocarbon dating**. Turns out, the landslide was more than 400 years older than the 1918 quake. Now scientists believe a series of faults in the nearby Mona Canyon, or rift, produced the quake and tsunami.

NAUTILUS

Uri ten Brink used the remotely operated vehicle called *Hercules*, above, and research ship *Nautilus*, left, to investigate the cause of the 1918 earthquake. These vessels were on loan from the Ocean Exploration Trust.

URI TEN BRINK AND THE USGS

Uri ten Brink is a scientist at the USGS and a professor at the University of Haifa in Israel. Through his work on the Puerto Rico Trench, he's provided the scientific community with a new understanding of the region's seismic activity.

Historically, the tectonics of the trench haven't been well understood because it's underwater and difficult to study. Brink warned in 2023 that it's important to learn more about the cause of earthquakes there because the region has many residents and tourists.

1787 BORICUA EARTHQUAKE

One of the strongest earthquakes ever recorded in Puerto Rico was the 1787 Boricua Earthquake. Residents reported feeling the quake all over the island, with significant damage everywhere but in the south. Most notably, the earthquake caused the walls of Our Lady of Guadalupe church in Ponce to crack. This church still stands but was damaged again in the 1918 earthquake.

Scientists aren't entirely sure where the epicenter of this earthquake was, but believe it was in the Puerto Rico Trench. They're also not sure about its strength. Some people believe it was 8.0 to 8.25 in magnitude, but others think it might have been a series of smaller, roughly 6.0-magnitude earthquakes instead of one larger one. The earthquake also caused a large tsunami to sweep over the land.

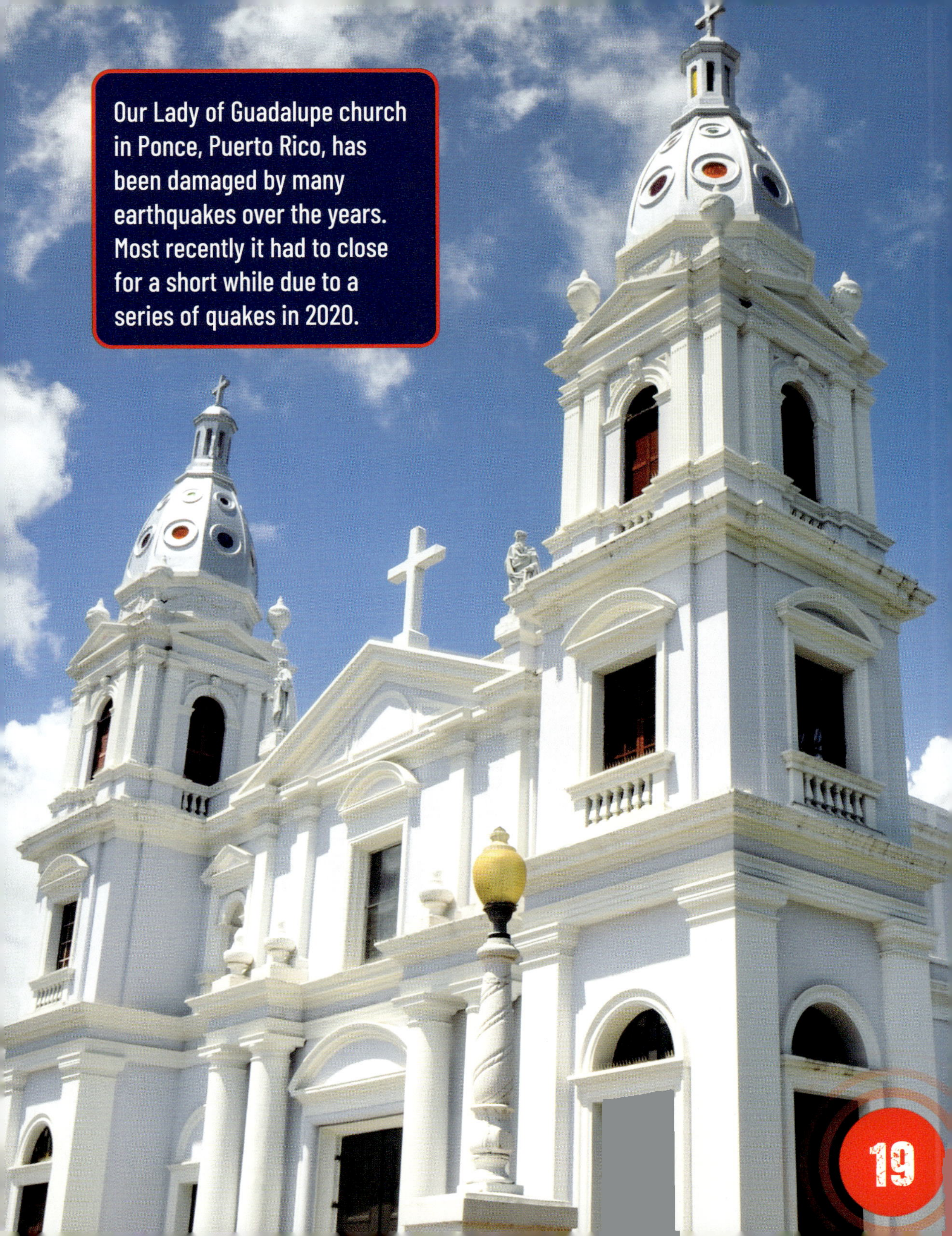

Our Lady of Guadalupe church in Ponce, Puerto Rico, has been damaged by many earthquakes over the years. Most recently it had to close for a short while due to a series of quakes in 2020.

PUERTO RICO SEISMIC NETWORK

Because earthquakes and tsunamis are such a threat to the people living near the Puerto Rico Trench, it's important for seismic activity there to be **monitored** constantly. One of the most important organizations doing this is the Puerto Rico Seismic Network (PRSN), part of the University of Puerto Rico's Department of Geology.

The USGS established the PRSN in 1974 to study seismic activity as the government prepared to build two nuclear power plants in Puerto Rico. Today, its goal is to provide important seismic data to scientists and emergency workers to better protect the population. The PRSN works with other government organizations as part of the TsunamiReady program to prepare people for the possibility of tsunamis, issue warnings, and provide **evacuation** signs and maps.

EARTH-SHAKING FACT!

When the PRSN issues a tsunami warning, it's safest for people to move farther inland and to higher ground.

This sign near a beach in Puerto Rico warns visitors that it's a possible tsunami zone.

MILWAUKEE DEEP

The Puerto Rico Trench is extremely deep. In fact, it's home to the deepest spot in the entire Atlantic Ocean. This spot is called Milwaukee Deep, named after the Navy's USS *Milwaukee*, which first identified the point in 1939. The trench's deepest point is about 28,000 feet (8,534 m) below sea level. The bottom of the Milwaukee Deep is covered in a rich sediment of mud, sand, rocks, and shells.

The USS *Milwaukee* was what the Navy called an Omaha-class light cruiser. During the time between the two World Wars, the ship was equipped with technology to explore the depths of the ocean.

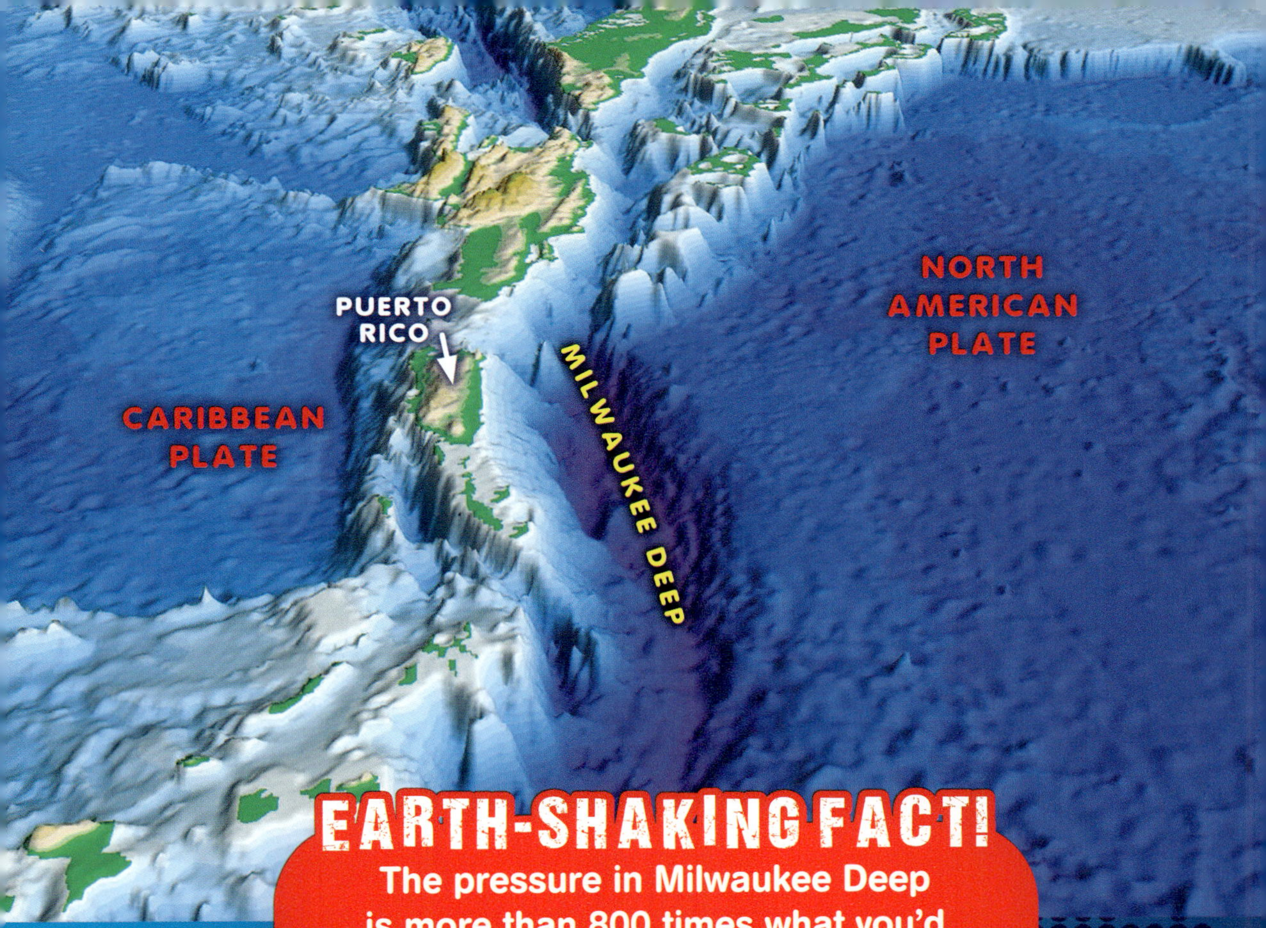

EARTH-SHAKING FACT!

The pressure in Milwaukee Deep is more than 800 times what you'd experience at sea level.

Humans can't go that far deep into the ocean without special protection. That's because the pressure from all that water above you would crush you. Amazingly, sea creatures have adapted to live at these incredible depths. Certain kinds of squid, eels, dragonfish, and other bizarre creatures can be found deep inside the Puerto Rico Trench.

FIVE DEEPS EXPEDITION

As the deepest point in the Atlantic Ocean, the Milwaukee Deep drew the attention of the Five Deeps Expedition. This was an effort led by American explorer Victor Vescovo to visit the deepest points in all five of the Earth's oceans. He completed this between December 2018 and August 2019.

His first dive? That would be to the Milwaukee Deep in the Atlantic Ocean. Vescovo was the first human to reach the deepest point in the Atlantic Ocean using a small **submersible**. During this dive, his submersible, called the *Limiting Factor*, also set the record for the deepest-diving submersible in the world. The Discovery Channel filmed a documentary of Vescovo's efforts called *Expedition: Deep Planet*.

Vescovo used the submersible *Limiting Factor* to travel to the bottom of Milwaukee Deep.

DR. ALAN JAMIESON

Vescovo's Five Deeps Expedition wasn't just about having fun and setting records. There was also a lot of science going on. Vescovo took Scottish marine biologist Dr. Alan Jamieson on the expedition, too. Together, they mapped the bottom of the ocean floor and studied the rare animals that live at such extreme depths. Jamieson said they wanted to find out how seismic activity can influence marine life.

UNUSUAL GRAVITY

The Puerto Rico Trench is exceptional not only for being the deepest point in the Atlantic Ocean—it also has some unusual gravity. In fact, it has the most negative gravity on Earth, meaning objects fall faster here than anywhere else. Scientists call this a gravity anomaly.

Scientists theorize there is more gravity in this area because there's a large, dense mass under the trench. In 1977, scientist Peter Molnar proposed that the Earth's crust under the trench is much thicker and denser than the crust elsewhere.

So, what does this unusual downward force mean? The change in gravity is so slight, humans don't notice it. But it can affect navigation equipment, which sailors rely on to travel safely through the Caribbean Sea.

EARTH-SHAKING FACT!

There are also positive gravity anomalies where gravity is weaker. The biggest one is in an area of the Indian Ocean.

This illustration shows the Earth's gravity. Areas of dark blue are negative gravity anomalies, while dark red areas are positive gravity anomalies.

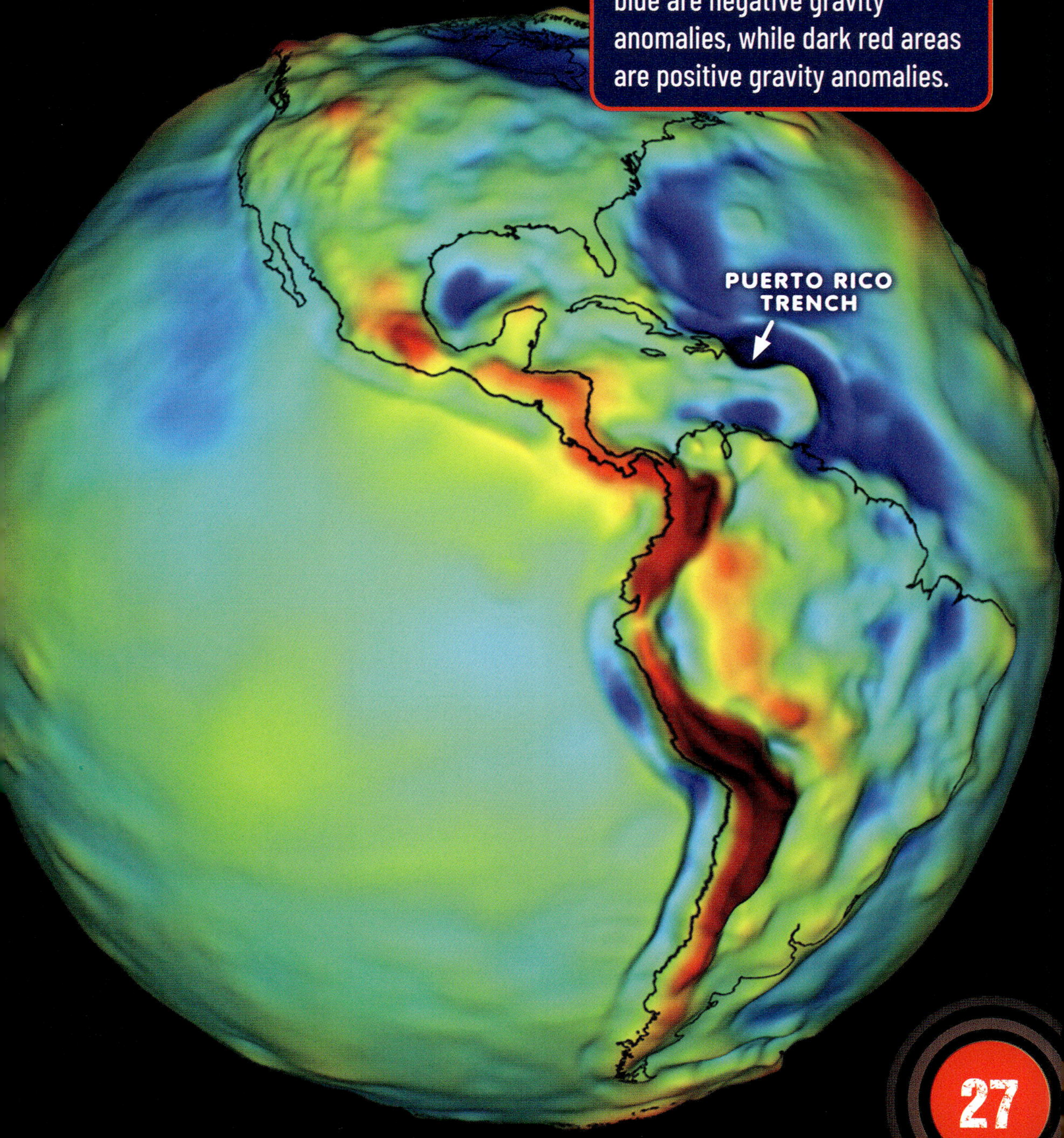

SEISMIC HOTSPOT

The Puerto Rico Trench is a mysterious place that has a lot to teach scientists about plate tectonics and gravity. But it also continues to be a danger to the people who live near it—Puerto Rico, the U.S. Virgin Islands, and other islands of the Caribbean.

This region faces the threat of highly destructive earthquakes and tsunamis at any time, and not just from the area of the trench. There are other seismic forces throughout the Caribbean—including active volcanoes and submarine landslides—that also pose a threat. That's all the more reason for scientists to continue to monitor the region and learn as much as they can about the plate tectonics that move our world.

EARTH-SHAKING FACT!

More than 4 million people live in the U.S. territories of Puerto Rico and the U.S. Virgin Islands. Both are also very popular with tourists from all over the world.

Puerto Rico is one of the most unusual places in the United States. Its location near the Puerto Rico Trench, though, puts this beautiful island territory at great risk.

GLOSSARY

aftershock: An earthquake that follows a stronger, primary earthquake.

epicenter: The point on Earth's surface directly above the center of an earthquake.

erode: To wear away the Earth's surface by wind or water.

evacuation: The process of leaving a place.

geological: Having to do with the study of rocks and Earth.

lava: Hot, liquid or soft rock above the surface of Earth.

magma: Hot, liquid or soft rock below the surface of Earth.

monitor: To observe and check the progress of something.

oblique: Having a slanting direction or position.

radiocarbon dating: The act of determining the age of something by measuring the amount of radioactive carbon it has.

significant: Very important.

submersible: A device designed for underwater work or exploration.

tectonic: Dealing with the structure of the Earth's crust.

theorize: To suggest an idea as possibly true but that is not known or proven to be true.

FOR MORE INFORMATION

BOOKS

Earley, Christina. *Plate Tectonics.* Coral Springs, FL: Seahorse Publishing, 2024.

Keppeler, Jill. *Earthquakes.* Buffalo, NY: Rosen Publishing, 2023.

Levy, Janey. *Puerto Rico.* Buffalo, NY: PowerKids Press, 2025.

WEBSITES

Britannica Kids: Plate Tectonics
www.kids.britannica.com/kids/article/plate-tectonics/346101
Read more about plate tectonics and how they shape our Earth.

Britannica Kids: Puerto Rico
www.kids.britannica.com/kids/article/Puerto-Rico/346196
Learn what makes this U.S. territory so special.

INDEX